THE
FANTASTIC
KINGDOM

THE
FANTASTIC
KINGDOM

Edited by David Larkin

With biographical notes by Margaret Maloney

Ballantine Books   New York

We gratefully acknowledge the following publishers
for permission to reproduce from their editions.

HODDER & STOUGHTON

WILLIAM HEINEMANN

DODD, MEAD & CO.

ALFRED A. KNOPF

BRENTANO'S

HARPER & BROTHER

JAMES NISBET & CO.

FREDERICK SAKS CO.

DUCKWORTH & CO.

To Kay and Sally

345   24242-4-495

Printed in Italy by Mondadori, Verona
This edition published by Ballantine Books
201 East 50th Street, New York, N.Y. 10022.

olklore, Myth, Fantasy — the very stuff of childhood. Often primitive in origin and violent in form, it still evokes deep sympathetic responses in all of us. These illustrators have caught this magic and present it in a highly polished form. While the pictures obviously illuminate the tales that inspired them, each stands alone as an intriguing and magical vision. These visual fantasies, ranging from whimsical to satirical, may be selected from children's book illustrations, but they still have universal appeal.

Many of the artists represented here have lapsed into obscurity and their original paintings have long been lost. Their work suffered because of poor reproduction, and we can only guess at what could have been achieved had they had the advantages of today's sophisticated technology. Despite the limitations of the then newly developed photographic half-tone printing processes, often restricted to only three colors, these illustrators form a surprisingly homogeneous group as they conjure up a very tangible world of make-believe.

Although Art Nouveau is one of the more readily discernible influences in their work, it is in no way dominant or pervasive. Each artist captures the elusive truth in fantasy, and therefore continues to captivate long after childhood ends.

losely identified with juvenile portraits and interpretations of child life, the Philadelphian **Jessie Willcox Smith** (1863-1935) fell rather accidentally upon her vocation. Following her natural attraction for and interest in children, she was studying to become a kindergarten teacher. In the days when propriety was rigorously observed, she agreed to join, as chaperone, a drawing class being given by a female friend at a local boys' school. When her impromptu sketches revealed startling promise, she transferred to the Philadelphia Academy of Fine Art, where she studied with Eakins. Later she worked at the Drexel Institute under the exacting Howard Pyle, who exerted a considerable influence on her style and through whom she secured her first book illustration assignment. Her idealized, romanticized pictures of children and flowers were soon in constant demand for cover and calendar designs, advertisements, and stories from such widely circulating publications as *Scribner's, Harper's, Collier's, St Nicholas, Ladies' Home Journal* and *Good Housekeeping*. Of her illustrations for children's classics, those for *The Water Babies* are considered among her finest.

PLATE 3

oward Pyle (1853-1911) was born of New England Quaker stock in Wilmington, Delaware, where his father owned a leather business. His mother brought him up on good books and quality illustration and was the primary force in fostering her son's dual literary and artistic talents. Restricted family finances fortuitously saved Pyle from the conventional 'polishing' in European ateliers and also from the Philadelphia Academy of Fine Art. Instead he studied under the Belgian-trained Van der Weilen in a small class, where his technique was improved and his individuality defined. He excelled in overlapping history and legend, drawing upon memories of his quiet, idyllic childhood, interwoven with America's colonial past. Tales of pirates fascinated Pyle: he spent holidays at Rehoboth, a seaside town whose neighboring sand dunes allegedly hid caches of stolen treasure, and these intrigues were reinforced by a trip to the West Indies and constant reading on the subject. His fellow artist, Frederic Remington, was an ardent admirer of his swashbuckling heroes. *Howard Pyle's Book of Pirates* is comprised of scattered selections, collected and published posthumously by his friend, Merle Johnson.

An English contemporary, Walter Crane, preferred the ornate medievalism of Pyle's *Merry Adventures of Robin Hood* (1883), considered by many his finest achievement, and the four-volume cycle of Arthurian romance. The acceptance of an illustrated article by *Scribner's Monthly* in 1876 initiated Pyle's career. Upon moving to New York city he soon became a regular contributor to popular magazines. *St Nicholas* paid him the modest fee of $2.50 for each illustrated fable or short story. He was befriended by Winslow Homer, Edwin Abbey and A. B. Frost. In 1894 Pyle turned to teaching, at the Drexel Institute in Philadelphia, and offered free summer classes to a select group of students at Chadd's Ford, Pennsylvania. By 1903 he had established another studio in an old grist-mill on the Brandywine River near his home in Wilmington, accepting only three out of almost three hundred applicants. Among those he inspired and challenged were Maxfield Parrish, N. C. Wyeth, and Jessie Willcox Smith. Through them Pyle's vigorous and original traditions were continued and diversified, making a deep and lasting impact on American illustration. Pyle was taken sick on his first trip abroad, and died suddenly in Florence.

PLATES 4, 5, 6, 7, 8, 9

 **rthur Rackham** (1867-1939), born in London, captioned a self-portrait in oils 'a transpontine Cockney'. One of twelve children, he displayed a precocious talent and a propensity for the fantastic. He drew constantly and, if forbidden paper, adorned pillows. Most of his ancestors were schoolmasters, and his father was a marshal in the British admiralty. Family tradition also held descent from a pirate, hanged in 1720 at Port Royal, Jamaica – a gruesomely romantic notion, which appealed strongly to the young boy's imagination. Rackham attended the Lambeth and Slade schools and studied in Paris. Charles Ricketts, a classmate, introduced him to the exotic, exaggerated motifs of Art Nouveau. Like George Cruikshank and Richard Doyle, Rackham combined in his style elements of humor, caricature and vitality, linked by an underlying humanness. While regularly employed first as an insurance officer, then as a journalistic illustrator, he submitted drawings to a number of publications. A commission to illustrate *Grimm's Fairy Tales* (1900) marked the beginning of his lasting fame. Several of his early works were originally done in black and white and then re-issued in color; some used

dramatic black silhouettes. A knowledgeable and practiced draftsman, Rackham restricted himself almost exclusively to book illustration, developing complete mastery of the complexities of the color plate. He closely followed the actual production process, altering colors – predominantly soft, muted grays and browns – if the proofs appeared inadequate. Meticulous and methodical, he believed that only the best was good enough. Incongruously, suggestions of terror mingled with fairy magic; he could create an incredibly hideous Caliban as easily as a breathtakingly ethereal Titania. His best-known subjects included *Rip Van Winkle* (1905), *Peter Pan in Kensington Gardens* (1906), and *Alice in Wonderland* (1907). By 1908 Rackham was elected a full member of the Royal Academy. The Teutonic imagery of Wagner's 'Ring' Cycle stirred him deeply. He often visited Germany and was an admirer of Dürer and Altdorfer. His wife, Edyth Starkie Rackham, was herself a gifted painter, as vivacious as he was reserved. However, he was fond of amateur theatricals, particularly Gilbert and Sullivan, for which he both acted and designed sets. In 1927 he toured the United States, where he was immensely popular. Walt Disney acknowledged emulating Rackham and tried to persuade him to come and work on the 1937 film production of *Snow White*. Pressure of other commitments had forced Rackham regretfully to decline an offer to illustrate the first edition of *The Wind in the Willows* (1908). Thirty years later, with laborious effort, he accomplished the task during his last losing battle against cancer.

PLATE 10

harles Robinson (1870-1937) was raised in North London. It is hardly surprising that he and his equally gifted brothers, Thomas and Heath, should have chosen artistic professions. Charles's grandfather had bound books at Newcastle-on-Tyne for the skilled and innovative wood-engraver Thomas Bewick, whose craft he made his own on coming to London; his father and uncle both drew for leading periodicals during the heyday of the wood-block illustration and developed literary and artistic associations in which the three boys took keen interest. Trained at the schools of the Royal Academy, Charles also served a seven-year apprenticeship in lithography. His first drawing was sold to Mr Joseph Darton, a prominent publisher of children's books. Robinson's illustrations for Robert Louis Stevenson's *A Child's Garden of Verses* (1896) established his reputation as a decorator *par excellence*. All three brothers collaborated on an elaborate and fanciful edition of *Fairy Tales from Hans Andersen* (1899). Charles preferred the black, rhythmically sinuous line of the Art Nouveau mode but also effectively used the opulent hues of Eastern art. For the amusement of his friends he drew menu cards and programmes in a Beardsleyesque manner, under the facetious pseudonym of 'Awfly Weirdley'.

rederick Maxfield Parrish (1870-1966) was born in Philadelphia into a creative atmosphere. As a youth he was exposed to European art while traveling with his father Stephen, a painter and etcher who regularly exhibited abroad. Originally intending to become an architect, Parrish enrolled at the Drexel Institute but was shortly dismissed by Howard Pyle, who considered him already too advanced to benefit. Winning national recognition in 1895 with a cover design for *Harper's Weekly*, he was soon on the way to becoming one of the best-paid American artists. He worked for magazines and advertising, selling literally millions of prints. Experimenting with photomontage, he placed epicene figures in surreal landscapes. He frequently painted from miniature models which he constructed himself, rearranging them in tentative composition. Belying his critics' charge of 'sentimentality', Parrish referred to himself as 'a mechanic who paints'. A rather chance occurrence had been responsible for his shift from a black-and-white to color medium: while recuperating from tuberculosis in the Adirondacks he found the sub-zero winter temperatures continually caused his ink to freeze and so he resorted to pigments thinned with oil. Although a vigorous contributor to the thriving turn-of-the-century poster trade, he stood apart from the fashion of Beardsley. Among Parrish's bookplate designs was one for the celebrated actress Ethel Barrymore. He did several large mural commissions based on nursery rhyme themes; 'King Cole' in the bar of the Knickerbocker Hotel was done for a fee of $50,000. However, romantic evocation remained his forte, and indeed his peril, in the commercial art game which demanded repetition of success. For thirteen years he churned out variant saccharine scenes of a pretty girl on a rock. Now, half a century later, 'pop art' promoters have rediscovered this master of the cliché. Parrish continued as an active artist until he was ninety-one.

PLATE 13

Destined to have his name become a dictionary entry, **William Heath Robinson** (1872-1944) was born in London, the youngest of three artistic brothers. He forsook early unsaleable attempts at painting, encouraged by his brothers' success to take up illustration. *Uncle Lubin*, his own juvenile fantasy, provided his first vehicle for surrealistic experiment. Needing a steady 'bread and butter' line to finance his marriage, Heath undertook commercial drawing, producing extravagant fantasies which marked a new departure in advertising. His involved contrivances, preposterous in conception, yet faultlessly logical in operation, amazed professional engineers. As a debunker of machine worship, his name became a byword for mechanical absurdity. During the First World War Robinson militarized his contraptions and caricatures. International acclaim threatened to engulf more serious opportunities; publishers were shocked at his long-held ambition to illustrate the life of Christ. A shy, preoccupied man, he worked intently, with feet wrapped around table legs and, according to friends, he was in constant danger from London traffic. In spite of his retiring disposition he was persuaded to undertake public appearances and broadcasting. He designed an exhibition home fitted with myriad gadgets. In collaboration with Kenneth R. G. Browne (son of artist Gordon and grandson of Dickens's illustrator, Hablot or 'Phiz'), Heath did a series of humorous 'how to —' handbooks. As a literary interpreter he showed an astonishing versatility, equally adept at capturing the macabre of Edgar Allan Poe, the buffoonery and ribaldry of Rabelais, and the delicacy, enchantment and whimsy of fairy tales. While in no way derivative, he adapted ideas from Beardsley and Sime as well as Crane, Greenaway and Rackham. Perrault's *Old-Time Stories* was his first major book commission after the war. He used modulated lighting, picked out with color points in beads, flowers, water, etc., in drawings which enrich rather than merely re-echo the theme. H. G. Wells counted Heath Robinson 'a joy in life' and Sir Kenneth Clark compared his ingenuity to that of Leonardo da Vinci.

PLATES 14, 15

elgian-born **Jean de Bosschère** (1881-1953) considered himself a 'strayed mystic' bound only by the creed of unconventionality. This poet of pen and brush possessed the vigor and violence, both grotesque and satiric, echoed from such sixteenth-century Gothic masters as Bosch and Breughel. In France he became a companion of the Symbolist poets, Paul Claudel and Paul Valéry, the latter appraising Bosschère's work as '*une différente magie, un instant de l'allusion murmurée de l'autre côté*'. Driven to London in 1915 in the wake of the war, he came in contact with Ezra Pound and T. S. Eliot. His two volumes of Flemish folk tales were rewritten from childhood memories. In addition to his own novels and poetry (occasionally written under the pseudonym J. P. Aubertin), Bosschère illustrated Rabelais, Flaubert, Baudelaire, Boccaccio and Oscar Wilde with a melancholy Gallic grace. One critic felt he was inspired by Freudian doctrines and should be considered from a psychological angle. His contemporary, Edmund Dulac, once presented him with a caricatured portrait in water colors.

PLATES 16, 17, 18, 19, 20, 21, 22, 23

fter unwillingly reading law, **Edmund Dulac** (1882-1953) switched to the Art School in his native Toulouse and later studied at the Académie Julian in Paris. He held annual shows at London's Leicester Galleries from 1907 to 1918 (with his drawings for the *Arabian Nights* holding pre-eminence). By 1912 he had settled permanently in London as a British subject. Dulac's inspiration was primarily oriental, with extravagant color harmonies reminiscent of Persian miniatures. Yet such seemingly disparate elements as the sinuous curves of Aubrey Beardsley, the flat, bold tones and flowing drapery of the newly popularized Japanese prints and the disembodied expressions preferred by the Pre-Raphaelites also blended aesthetically. Like his rival, Arthur Rackham, to whom he was fifteen years junior, Dulac contributed generously to fund-raising publications during World War II and became identified with the sumptuous, if ponderous and expensive, 'coffee-table' volumes with mounted color plates. His many-faceted artistry was revealed in portraits, caricatures (including wax dolls, one of which, Sir Thomas Beecham, is owned by the London Museum), stage sets and costumes for the theater. Other designs included a Free French banknote, several British and French postage stamps (the regular issue of George VI and the Coronation Commemorative of 1937), the King's Poetry Prize Medal, and a variety of playing cards.

PLATE 24

dward Julius Detmold, born in London in 1883, shared an equal facility for illustration and engraving with his twin brother, Charles Maurice, until the latter's tragic suicide by poison at twenty-five. The boys were educated by an uncle whose knowledge of natural history fostered their inherent inclination and aptitude. At thirteen they were already exhibiting at the Royal Academy. Edward Burne-Jones praised their work but advised against the restrictive routine of art school. They soon began experimenting with etching and saved money from their earliest sales to buy a printing press, from which they did their own proofs at home. Both were admirers of Dürer but were influenced considerably by the current vogue of Japanese color-prints. They frequently collaborated on a single harmonious plate and jointly illustrated Kipling's *The Jungle Book* (1903). After his brother's death Edward Julius continued illustrating animals, insects and plants usually in water-colors, for the gift book trade, and did wood and copper engraving. His subjects, while biologically accurate in detail, were often placed in a surrealistic setting or incongruous juxtaposition, creating a dreamlike phenomenon.

PLATE 25

**etermined** to become a serious artist, **Paul Bransom** (born 1885) left school at fourteen and began work as a patent draftsman in his native Washington, D.C. By eighteen he had headed for New York and a more creative career, specializing in the depiction of wild-life. He contributed to a whimsical newspaper comic strip called 'The News from Bugville' but spent all his free time avidly sketching at the city's two major zoos. Through Dr William Hornaday he gained the rare privilege of a studio situated right in the New York Zoological Park. His first real opportunity came with four animal-study covers for the *Saturday Evening Post*, followed shortly by his initial book commission for Jack London's bestseller, *The Call of the Wild* (1912). The following year he illustrated Kenneth Grahame's classic, *The Wind in the Willows*, and was later associated with several works by Charles G. D. Roberts. For many years Bransom spent the summer in the Adirondack Mountains, drawing animals in their natural habitat. In 1948 he espoused the life of the small rancher in Wyoming, painting the scenery and fauna of the American West.

PLATES 26, 27, 28, 29, 30, 31, 32

Also nurtured in a receptive environment was **Kay Nielsen** (1886-1957). His father was a classical actor in his youth and later a director of the Dagmartheater, Copenhagen; his mother was an actress to the court of the royal Danish theater. Youthful recollections included such personalities as Ibsen, Björnson, Grieg, and Lie. He would illustrate the traditional folklore and sagas as they were read aloud by his mother. The tone and texture of drawings and carvings brought home from China by his maternal grandfather fascinated Nielsen. Privately tutored from the age of twelve, he considered a medical career, but at seventeen left formal study for first-hand experience in the Montparnasse section of Paris, where he began sketching in black and white. After attending the Académies Julian and Colarossis, he moved to London from 1911 to 1916 and held his first American show in 1917. Settling in Los Angeles in 1939, he worked as an actor, director, set designer and muralist until his death in Hollywood. Much of his illustration was touched by the exquisite bizarrerie of Art Nouveau motifs.

PLATES 33, 34, 35, 36

A **little known** but highly individualistic craftsman in the Art Nouveau stream was the imaginative and erudite Irishman, **Harry Clarke** (1890-1931). Abandoning an early interest in medicine, at sixteen he became apprenticed to his father, who controlled a large and reputable stained glass firm in Dublin. Upon resuming his artistic studies, Clarke won gold medals in three consecutive years and in 1913 was commended by such established artists and teachers as Walter Crane and Byam Shaw. He was awarded a traveling scholarship to study the cathedral windows of the Ile de France. Examples of his own subsequent work can be found in many churches in Eire, England, Wales, Australia and Africa. He designed textiles in addition to book illustration. His style ranged from the bizarre fantasy, verging on horror, of his Beardsleyesque patterns for Poe's *Tales of Mystery and Imagination* or Goethe's *Faust* to the delicacy and orderliness of his fresh conception of Perrault's fairy tales. Clarke's rich and versatile talent was destroyed by tuberculosis, for he died in Switzerland at the premature age of forty.

**orothy Pulis Lathrop** was born in Albany, New York, in 1891. The early influence of her artist mother and her paternal grandfather, who ran a bookshop in Connecticut, made illustration and literature focal points in her life. While attending Vassar College she intended to pursue a writing career but was swayed, by economic exigencies, to favor art instead. She studied with Arthur Dow and afterwards Henry McCarter and F. Luis Mora, and began illustrating in 1918. The first book for which Miss Lathrop did the text as well as the pictures was *The Fairy Circus* (1931). Animals remained her preferred and best-realized subjects, drawn usually from the live models provided by her household pets. Among many awards she has received was the first presentation of the Caldecott Medal for *Animals of the Bible* (1938). For many years she shared a studio with her sister Gertrude, a noted sculptor.

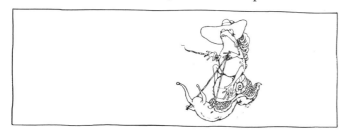

PLATE 40

**ery little** can be discovered about the elusive **T. Mackenzie** beyond the facts that he was an Englishman working in the early decades of the twentieth century, sufficiently accomplished to warrant a commission to illustrate an elaborate and obviously expensive limited folio edition of a long narrative poem, *Aladdin and His Wonderful Lamp*, by the novelist Arthur Ransome; it was printed on hand-made vellum, with mounted plates, and the illustrator effectively employed designs and colors assimilated from Art Nouveau and Eastern prints. But after that he seems to have vanished, without a trace, from the artistic world.

The Editor is grateful to
the Chief Librarian of The Toronto Public Library
and the Staff at Boys and Girls House
for their help and co-operation in
the preparation of this book.

1) He felt how comfortable it was to have nothing on him but himself.

JESSIE WILLCOX SMITH
The Water Babies

HODDER & STOUGHTON
1919

2) Mrs. Doasyouwouldbedoneby

JESSIE WILLCOX SMITH

HODDER & STOUGHTON

1919

3) An attack on a Galleon.

HOWARD PYLE

Howard Pyle's Book of Pirates

HARPER & BROTHER

1921

4) Mime at the anvil

ARTHUR RACKHAM
Siegfried and the Twilight of the Gods

WILLIAM HEINEMANN
1911

5) Siegfried kills Fafner

ARTHUR RACKHAM
Siegfried and the Twilight of the Gods

WILLIAM HEINEMANN
1911

6) Seize the despoiler! Rescue the gold! Help us! Help us! Woe! Woe!

ARTHUR RACKHAM

The Rhinegold and the Valkyrie

WILLIAM HEINEMANN

1910

7) Waken, Waken, Burd Ishel.

ARTHUR RACKHAM
Some Ballads

DODD, MEAD & CO.
1919

8) Ohe! Ohe! Horrible the Dragon, O swallow me not!
Spare the life of poor 'Loge'

ARTHUR RACKHAM

The Rhinegold and the Valkyrie

WILLIAM HEINEMANN

1910

9) The Rhine's fair children bewailing their lost gold, weep.

ARTHUR RACKHAM

The Rhinegold and the Valkyrie

WILLIAM HEINEMANN

1910

CHARLES ROBINSON

10) The Russian Princess.

CHARLES ROBINSON
The Happy Prince and Other Stories
DUCKWORTH & CO.
1913

11) No blue nor red was ever seen,
so amorous as this lovely green,
here at the fountain's sliding foot
or at some fruit-tree's mossy root,
casting the body's vest aside
my soul into the boughs does glide.

MAXFIELD PARRISH

A Golden Treasury of Songs and Lyrics

DODD, MEAD & CO.
1911

12) How sweet the answer Echo makes
to music at night when,
roused by lute or horn, she wakes
and far away o'er lawns and lakes
goes answering light!

MAXFIELD PARRISH

A Golden Treasury of Songs and Lyrics

DODD, MEAD & CO.

1911

13) They reached the house where the light was burning.

W. HEATH ROBINSON
Old Time Stories

DODD, MEAD & CO.
1921

14) The Devil beaten three times.

JEAN DE BOSSCHÈRE
Christmas Tales of Flanders

WILLIAM HEINEMANN
1917

15) The Dwarf's Feast
JEAN DE BOSSCHÈRE
Christmas Tales of Flanders
WILLIAM HEINEMANN
1917

16) *Dahnash and Meymooneh.*

'As she rose up through the clouds there passed
one she knew by his tail to be Dahnash'.

EDMUND DULAC

Princess Badoura, A Tale from the Arabian Nights

HODDER & STOUGHTON

1913

17) And her Godmother pointed to the finest of all with her wand.

EDMUND DULAC

The Sleeping Beauty and Other Fairy Tales

HODDER & STOUGHTON

1910

18) Ah! What a fright you gave me! She murmured.
EDMUND DULAC
The Sleeping Beauty and Other Fairy Tales
HODDER & STOUGHTON
1910

19) *The Buried Moon*

In her frantic struggles, the hood of her cloak
fell back from her dazzling golden hair,
and immediately the whole place was flooded with light.

EDMUND DULAC
Edmund Dulac's Fairy Book

HODDER & STOUGHTON
1916

20) *The Blue Bird*

The Prince took a carriage drawn by three great frogs with
great wings . . . Fruitonni came out mysteriously by a little door.

EDMUND DULAC

Edmund Dulac's Fairy Book

HODDER & STOUGHTON

1916

21) *The Story of Bashtchelik*
The Palace of the Dragon King
EDMUND DULAC
Edmund Dulac's Fairy Book
HODDER & STOUGHTON
1915

22) The Eagle in the great forest flew swiftly,
but the Eastwind flew more swiftly still.

EDMUND DULAC

Stories from Hans Anderson

HODDER & STOUGHTON

1911

23) His limbs were numbed, his beautiful eyes were closing,
and he must have died if the little mermaid
had not come to the rescue.

EDMUND DULAC

Stories from Hans Anderson

HODDER & STOUGHTON

1911

24) The Owl and the Birds
EDWARD J. DETMOLD
Fables of Aesop
HODDER & STOUGHTON
1909

25) The frog took a sudden plunge to the bottom.

PAUL BRANSOM

An Argosy of Fables

FREDERICK SAKS CO.

1921

26) The North Wind goes over the sea

KAY NEILSEN

East of the Sun, West of the Moon

HODDER & STOUGHTON

1913

27) And flitted away as far as they could
from the Castle that lay
East of the Sun and West of the Moon

KAY NEILSEN
East of the Sun, West of the Moon

HODDER & STOUGHTON
1913

28) He took a long, long farewell of the Princess,
and when he got out of the Giant's door,
there stood the Wolf waiting for him.

KAY NEILSEN

East of the Sun, West of the Moon

HODDER & STOUGHTON

1914

29) The Lad in the Battle
KAY NEILSEN
East of the Sun, West of the Moon
HODDER & STOUGHTON
1914

30) The Troll was quite willing,
and before long he fell asleep and began snoring.

KAY NEILSEN

East of the Sun, West of the Moon

HODDER & STOUGHTON

1914

31) The King went into the Castle,
and at first his Queen didn't know him, he was so wan and thin,
through wandering so far and being so woeful.

KAY NEILSEN

East of the Sun, West of the Moon

HODDER & STOUGHTON

1914

32) When the Cock Crowed.

KAY NEILSEN

In Powder and Crinoline

HODDER & STOUGHTON

1912

33) Let him have his head cut off!
HARRY CLARKE
Hans Christian Anderson

BRENTANO'S
1916

34) Have you really the courage to go into the wide world with me?
asked the chimney sweep.

HARRY CLARKE

Hans Christian Anderson

BRENTANO'S

1916

35) On the grave of the Prince's father there grew a rosebush.

HARRY CLARKE

Hans Christian Anderson

BRENTANO'S

1916

36) Kay and the Snow Queen.
HARRY CLARKE
Hans Christian Anderson
BRENTANO'S
1916

37) He in turn, leaning over the rock stared back
into Martin's face with his immense fishy eyes.

DOROTHY P. LATHROP

Little Boy Lost

ALFRED A. KNOPF

1920

38) He felt a sudden darkness above his head,
and a cold terror crept over his skin.

DOROTHY P. LATHROP

The Three Mulla Mulgars

DUCKWORTH & CO.

1921

39) Oh, but if I might hold it in my hand one moment,
I think that I should never even sigh again!

DOROTHY P. LATHROP
The Three Mulla Mulgars

DUCKWORTH & CO.
1921

40) A crowd of pig-tailed Chinamen who bowed.

T. MACKENZIE

Aladdin and His Wonderful Lamp

JAMES NISBET & CO.

1919